# Kids Can Draw
# FAVORITE PETS

by Philippe Legendre

*Walter Foster*

© 1997, 2002 Editions Fleurus, Paris.
Text on pages 4–24 © 1997, 2002 Walter Foster Publishing, Inc. All rights reserved.
Original title *J'apprends à dessiner les animaux de la maison*, © 1992 Editions Fleurus, Paris.

## Attention Parents and Teachers

All children can draw a circle, a square, or a triangle…which means that they can also learn to draw a poodle, cat, or turtle! The KIDS CAN DRAW learning method is easy and fun. Children will learn a technique and a vocabulary of shapes that will form the basis for all kinds of drawing.

Pictures are created by combining geometric shapes to form a mass of volumes and surfaces. From this stage, children can give character to their sketches with straight, curved, or broken lines.

With just a few strokes of the pencil, a favorite pet will appear—and with the addition of color, the picture will be real work of art!

The KIDS CAN DRAW method offers a real apprenticeship in technique and a first look at composition, proportion, shapes, and lines. The simplicity of this method ensures that the pleasure of drawing is always the most important factor.

## About Philippe Legendre

French painter, engraver, and illustrator, Philippe Legendre also runs a school of art for children aged 6–14 years. Legendre frequently spends time in schools and has developed this method of learning so that all children can discover the artist within themselves.

## Helpful Tips

1. Each picture is made up of simple geometric shapes, which are illustrated at the top of the left-hand page. This is called the **Vocabulary of Shapes.** Encourage children to practice drawing each shape before starting their pictures.

2. Suggest children use a pencil to do their sketches. This way, if they don't like a particular shape, they can just erase it and try again.

3. A dotted line indicates that the line should be erased. Have children draw the whole shape and then erase the dotted part of the line.

4. Once children finish their drawings, they can color them with crayons, colored pencils, or felt-tip markers. They may want to go over the lines with a black pencil or pen.

## Now let's get started!

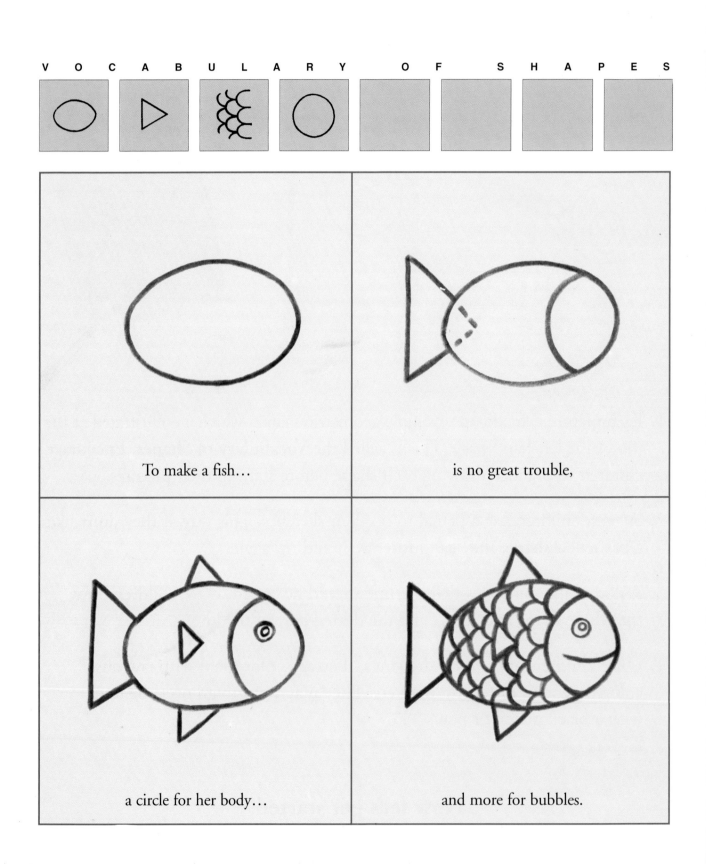

To make a fish…

is no great trouble,

a circle for her body…

and more for bubbles.

# Fish

If you draw…

some curly doodles,

soon you'll see…

a fluffy poodle.

# Poodle

A circle makes…

the head atop…

a bunny that…

goes hippity-hop.

# Bunny

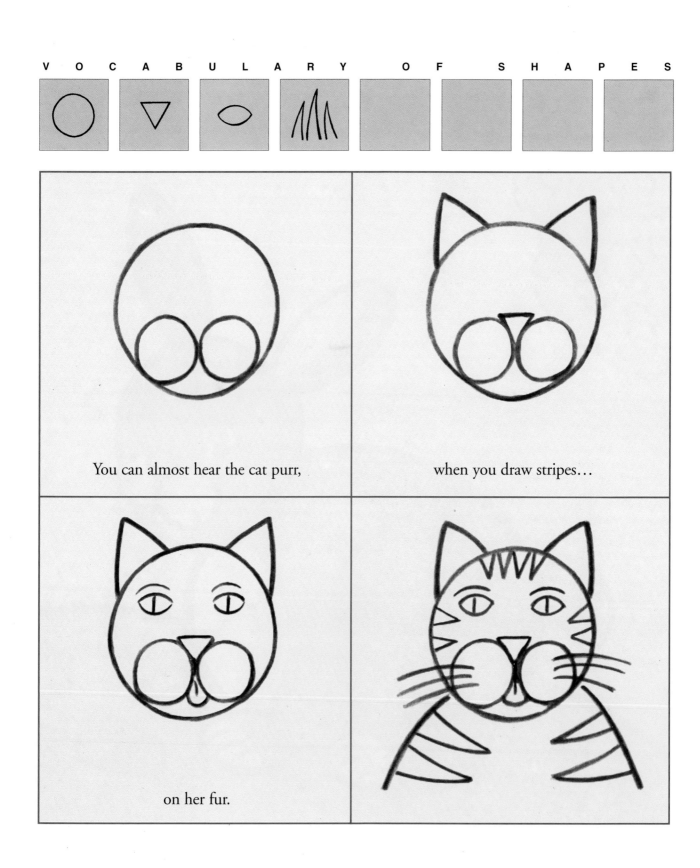

You can almost hear the cat purr,

when you draw stripes…

on her fur.

# Cat

His bumpy shell…

with squares is packed.

He carries his home…

upon his back.

# Turtle

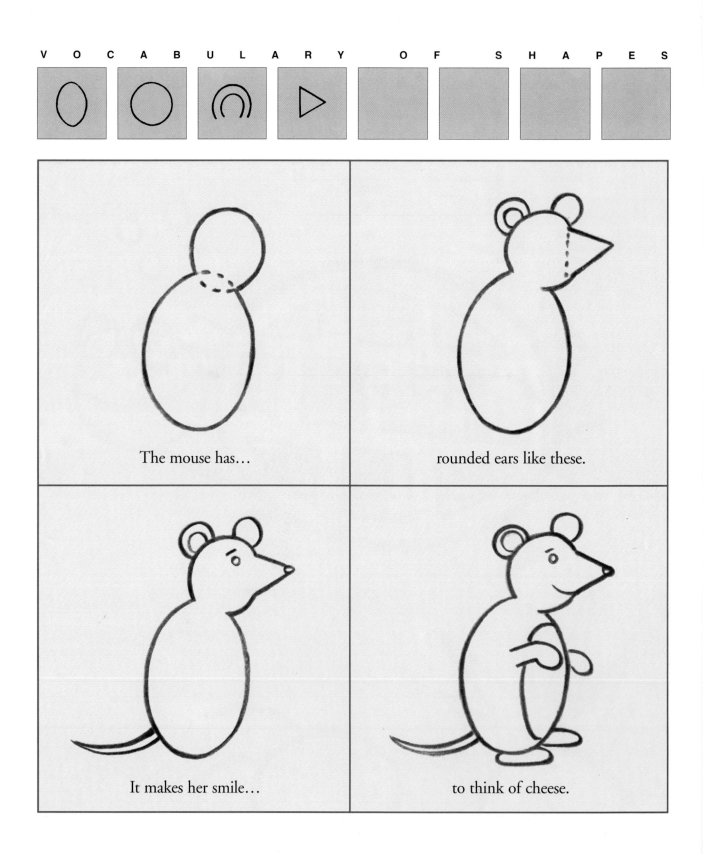

The mouse has...

rounded ears like these.

It makes her smile...

to think of cheese.

# **M**ouse

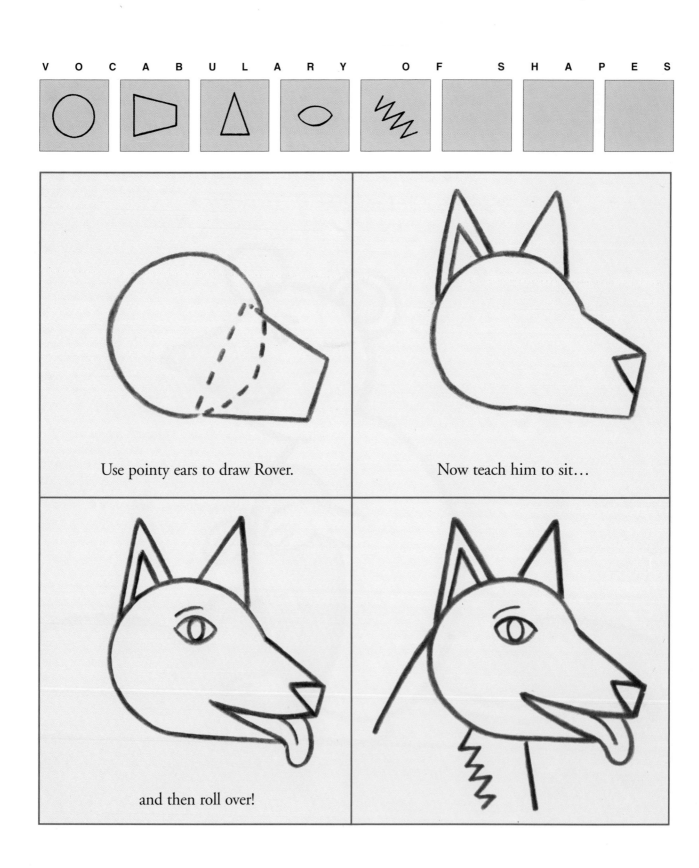

Use pointy ears to draw Rover.

Now teach him to sit…

and then roll over!

# Dog

To draw this furry fellow,

make a half-circle big.

But don't draw a curly tail—

he's not a real pig!

# Guinea Pig

This brightly colored bird…

has triangles for feet.

"Polly wants a cracker,"

says the parakeet.

# Parakeet

At last, you can draw your favorite pets—from a trusty dog to a little mouse.

Now make a pretty picture of them living in your house.

# Draw-along fun for children!

With the "I Can Draw" series, kids ages 6 and up will have hours of fun drawing amazing pictures of the things they like best—animals, cartoons, creepy creatures, race cars, and more. Each book is full of colorful step-by-step illustrations with easy-to-follow instructions. Kids will learn how to draw almost anything by starting with the basic shapes they already know, such as circles, squares, triangles, and ovals. Each 40-page book includes 8 pages of grid paper.

## Walter Foster

For a free catalog, write to Walter Foster Publishing, Inc.
23062 La Cadena Drive, Laguna Hills, CA 92653
800/426-0099 • www.walterfoster.com